Step Inside a Story

Plays by Julia Donaldson

Illustrated by Gerald Kelley

The Author Visit 3

Jack and the Author 18

Published by Pearson Education Limited, Edinburgh Gate, Harlow, Essex, CM20 2JE.

www.pearsonschools.co.uk

Text © Julia Donaldson 2013

Designed by Georgia Styring
Original illustrations © Pearson Education 2013
Illustrated by Gerald Kelley, The Bright Agency
Cover design by Gerald Kelley

The right of Julia Donaldson to be identified as author of this work has been
asserted by her in accordance with the Copyright, Designs and Patents Act 1988.

First published 2013

17

10 9 8 7 6 5

British Library Cataloguing in Publication Data
A catalogue record for this book is available from the British Library

ISBN 978 0 435 14427 2

Printed and bound by Golden Cup

Acknowledgements
We would like to thank Bangor Central Integrated Primary School, Northern Ireland;
Bishop Henderson Church of England Primary School, Somerset; Bletchingdon
Parochial Church of England Primary School, Oxfordshire; Brookside Community
Primary School, Somerset; Bude Park Primary School, Hull; Carisbrooke Church
of England Primary School, Isle of Wight; Cheddington Combined School,
Buckinghamshire; Dair House Independent School, Buckinghamshire; Deal Parochial
School, Kent; Glebe Infant School, Goucestershire; Henley Green Primary School,
Coventry; Lovelace Primary School, Surrey; Our Lady of Peace Junior School, Slough;
Tackley Church of England Primary School, Oxfordshire; and Twyford Church of
England School, Buckinghamshire for their invaluable help in the development and
trialling of the Bug Club resources.

Photo of Julia Donaldson by Alex Rumford

Every effort has been made to contact copyright holders of material reproduced in
this book. Any omissions will be rectified in subsequent printings if notice is given to
the publishers.

The Author Visit

Characters

Teacher

Ruby Wright

Ivor Brush

Emily

Connor

Rory

Teacher: Now, children, we're very lucky to have two visitors today. This is the famous author, Miss Ruby Wright. She wrote 'The Purple Penguin' and lots of other books.

Ruby: It's wonderful to be here.

Teacher: And this is Ruby's illustrator, Mr Ivor Brush.

Ivor: Hello.

Teacher: Who can remember what an illustrator is?

Rory: It's someone who has an illness.

Teacher: No, Rory.

Emily: It's the person who draws the pictures.

Teacher: That's right, Emily. Now, I'm sure you all have lots of questions. Connor's got his hand up already.

Connor: Where do you get your ideas?

Ruby: Well, my books are about animals, so sometimes I go to the zoo to get ideas.

Teacher: How fascinating. And who has a question for Ivor? Yes, Emily?

Emily: Do you go to the zoo to draw the animals?

Ivor: No – I use my imagination.

Teacher: That's just what I keep telling the children to do! Any more questions? Yes, Rory?

Rory: My dad had a fight with a polar bear.

Teacher: Don't be silly, Rory. Anyway, that's not a question.

Connor: What's your favourite book, Ruby?

Ruby: I think it's probably 'The Orange Ostrich'.

Emily: What's that about?

Ruby: It's about an ostrich who doesn't fit in with the other ostriches because he's not the same colour.

Connor: Do you like drawing ostriches, Ivor?

Ivor: Not especially. Well, not orange ones, anyway. But I have to draw whatever Ruby writes about.

Teacher: Who else has a question?

Rory: My cat's called Sooty.

Teacher: That's not a question; it's a statement. Anyone else?

Emily: What's your favourite colour, Ruby? Is it orange?

Ruby: No, actually it's green. My new book is going to be called 'The Green Gorilla'.

Connor: What's that one about?

Ruby: It's about a gorilla who doesn't fit in with the others ...

Ivor: ... because he's not the same colour as them. All her books are like that.

Emily: What's your favourite colour, Ivor?

Ivor: It's turquoise, but unfortunately Ruby never writes about any turquoise animals.

Ruby: Some people are never happy!

Teacher: Who has a question about books?

Rory: I've got a book about aliens.

Teacher: Rory, that's not a question. Who has an actual question?

Connor: How long does it take to write a book?

Ruby: Well, every book is different. But 'The Orange Ostrich' was one of the quickest because I was so inspired. It only took about a week.

Emily: How long did it take to do the pictures, Ivor?

Ivor: About a year, but that was because Ruby kept telling me to change things.

Ruby: Well, your ostriches looked more like vultures!

Teacher: Do you like being an author, Ruby?

Ruby: Yes, I love it! I'm so lucky to be paid to do my favourite thing – writing about animals.

Emily: Do you like being an illustrator, Ivor?

Ivor: Er ... yes. But I **would** like to draw some people for a change.

Rory: My mum says there are more than seven billion people in the world.

Teacher: Any more questions?

Connor: Do you get paid a lot of money?

Emily: Yes, do you get the same amount each?

Teacher: You shouldn't really ask questions like that.

Ruby: That's all right. Yes, we do get paid the same, even though I'm the one who comes up with all the ideas. I mean, Ivor could never have thought of a blue boa-constrictor or a red rhino.

Ivor: Thank goodness.

Ruby: I think Ivor is just a teeny bit jealous!

Rory: It's my Granny's birthday today.

Ivor: If anything, I should get paid more than Ruby because her stories are so difficult to illustrate.

Ruby: Nonsense! You're just not very good at it. That yellow yak of yours looked more like a dinosaur.

Ivor: That's it! I'm not taking any more of this. And I'm not going to illustrate any more of your books!

Ivor exits.

Ruby: Ivor, don't be like that! I was only joking!

Rory: I know loads of elephant jokes.

Ruby: Oh dear. Ivor, Ivor! COME BACK!

Ruby runs out after Ivor.

16

Teacher: Well, that was interesting, wasn't it?

Connor: Can we do some creative writing now, Miss?

Emily: Or can we do art?

Teacher: No, I think we'll do some sums.

Jack and the Author

Characters

Author

Jack's Mother

Giantess

Golden Hen

Giant

Jack

Author: Once upon a time, there was a boy called Jack.

Jack: That's me. I'm very brave.

Author: Jack lived with his mother ...

Mother: That's me. I'm a really good cook.

Author: This always happens! As soon as I start writing, my characters come to life.

Mother: I made this lovely bean stew last night, and ...

Author: Stop interrupting! Meanwhile, up in the clouds, there lived a giant.

Giant: Fee, fi, fo, fum!

Author: You're not supposed to say that yet. The giant had a wife.

Giantess: That's me. Can't you say "a beautiful wife"?

Author: All right – a beautiful wife. And a golden hen.

Hen: That's me. Can I sing my song now?

Author: No, not yet. One day, Jack woke up to find a beanstalk growing outside his window.

Jack: Yes, and I bravely climbed up it!

Mother: Why should Jack have all the adventures? I want to climb it.

Author: Oh, all right then. Jack's mother climbed up the beanstalk.

Jack: That's ridiculous!

21

Author: At the top, she found an enormous castle.

Hen: Is it nearly time for my song?

Giant: No. I haven't said "Fee, fi, fo, fum" yet.

Giantess: It's my turn first.
(To Jack's mother)
Hello, dear, come in. Would you like a cup of tea?

Mother: Yes, please. That's a nice smell. What are you cooking?

Giantess: Bean curry. It's the giant's favourite.

Hen sings.

Hen: Run, giant, run, on your big long legs! Save the hen with the ...

Author: Be quiet, Hen! It's not time for your song yet.

Mother: No, we're still having our nice chat about curry. Can I have the recipe?

Giantess: Of course. I'll write it out for you.

Jack: This is all wrong!

Giant: Fee, fi, fo, fum! I smell the blood of an Englishman.

Giantess: It's not a man, dear, it's a woman.

Mother: And I'm only half English. My dad is Polish.

Giantess: Fancy that! Would you like to stay for lunch?

Mother: Thanks, but I'd better get back to Jack.

Hen: Aren't you going to steal me, first? Then I can sing my song.

Mother: Me, steal a hen? Certainly not. I'm not a thief!

Author: Er ... so Jack's mother climbed back down the beanstalk.

Jack: Well, that wasn't very exciting. Let me have a go.

Author: All right. The next day, Jack climbed up the beanstalk. He met the giant's wife and she hid him in the oven.

Giant: This is more like it.
Fee, fi, fo, fum!
I smell the blood of an English ... er,
or Polish ... man.
Be he alive or be he dead
I'll grind his bones to make my bread.

Giantess: Don't be silly, dear. You don't make bread out of bones!

Mother: I've got a really good book of bread recipes.

Jack: Be quiet, Mum. You're not in this bit.

Author: Jack grabbed the giant's golden hen and ran away.

Hen: Hooray! Now I can sing my song. Run, giant, run, on your big long legs! Save the hen with the golden eggs! With a cluck cluck here and a cluck cluck there. Here a cluck, there a cluck ...

Giant: That's not how it goes.

Author: Jack climbed back down the beanstalk.

Giant: I'm going after him!

Giantess: I wouldn't do that, dear. He might get an axe and chop it down. Why don't you have some nice curry instead?

Author: Jack's mother was delighted to see the hen.

Mother: No, I'm not. That's stealing, Jack! Take it straight back.

Jack: Oh, Mum!

Hen: Good! Now I can sing a new song. Climb, Jack, climb on your small short legs! Carry the hen with the golden eggs!

Mother: And while you're there, get me that recipe from the nice giant lady.

Author: So Jack climbed back up the beanstalk.

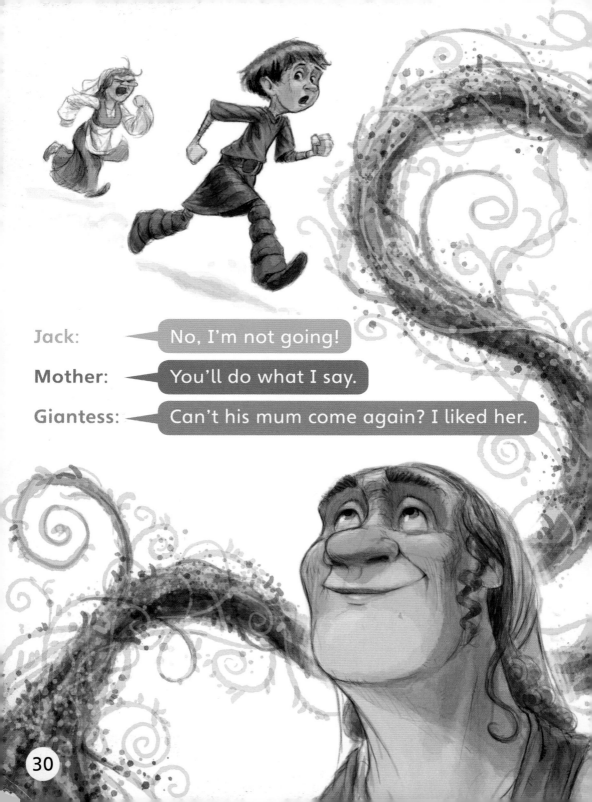

Jack: No, I'm not going!

Mother: You'll do what I say.

Giantess: Can't his mum come again? I liked her.

Giant: Fee, fi, fo, fum!

Hen: With a cluck cluck here and a cluck cluck there ...

Author: Oh, BE QUIET, you lot! I'm going to tear this story up and start a new one. Once upon a time ...